FILCHED

Poems by

JAMES TOLAN

DOS MADRES

2017

DOS MADRES PRESS INC.

P.O.Box 294, Loveland, Ohio 45140

www.dosmadres.com   editor@dosmadres.com

Dos Madres is dedicated to the belief that the small press is essential to the vitality of contemporary literature as a carrier of the new voice, as well as the older, sometimes forgotten voices of the past. And in an ever more virtual world, to the creation of fine books pleasing to the eye and hand.

Dos Madres is named in honor of Vera Murphy and Libbie Hughes, the "Dos Madres" whose contributions have made this press possible.

Dos Madres Press, Inc. is an Ohio Not For Profit Corporation and a 501 (c) (3) qualified public charity. Contributions are tax deductible.

Executive Editor: Robert J. Murphy

Illustration & Book Design: Elizabeth H. Murphy
www.illusionstudios.net

Front Cover Photo by Junuh Tolan

Typset in Adobe Garamond Pro & Engravers MT
ISBN 978-1-939929-79-2
Library of Congress Control Number: 2017933776

First Edition

ACKNOWLEDGMENTS

Thanks to the following, where these poems previously appeared:

The American Journal of Poetry: "Spikes Driven into Oak"
Big City Lit: "A Penniless Piece of Spent Fashion"
Connotation Press: "Terror in the Service of Delight" and
    "While I Complained—"
I-70 Review: "Fire and Water," "Hot Pants and the Guillotine,"
    "Leaving Home," and "Sunday in the Village"
J Journal: "Filched"
Linebreak: "Supposed to"
Midwestern Gothic: "A Wild Rumpus"
Montreal Review: "Mr. Waters and the Crackers"
New America: Contemporary Literature for a Changing Society:
    "The Big Sleep"
New Poetry from the Midwest: "Leaving Home"
Paterson Literary Review: "It was the 70's"
Ploughshares: "The Big Sleep"
Quarter after Eight: "The Egg Man, the Podiatrist, and Me"
Rattle Young Poets Anthology 2016: "Spirit"
Realms of the Mothers: Ten Years of Dos Madres Press: "Filched"
    and "It was the 70's"
Wake: "Tag"

"The Big Sleep," "Filched," "It was the 70's," and "A Penniless
Piece of Spent Fashion" are included in the chapbook *Red Walls*
(Dos Madres Press).

And so much gratitude to my wife, brilliant friends and teachers who
did so much to help improve many of these poems and their ar-
rangement: Holly Messitt, Fran Quinn, Cecilia Woloch, Olivia Stif-
fler, Owen Lewis, Dorianne Laux, Nicole Callahan, Lorraine Doran,
Myra Shapiro, Wendy Larsen, Maryann Downing. Deep felt thanks
as well to Robert and Elizabeth Murphy at Dos Madres Press, whose
roles in my life extend beyond belief in my work and the making of
beautiful books to giving me the gift of feeling like family.

for Holly and Junuh

Only with you did poetry return in its sweet ache and joy.

Now the inevitable
As in tales of woe
The inexorable toll
It takes, it takes.
                    —*Robert Creeley*

TABLE OF CONTENTS

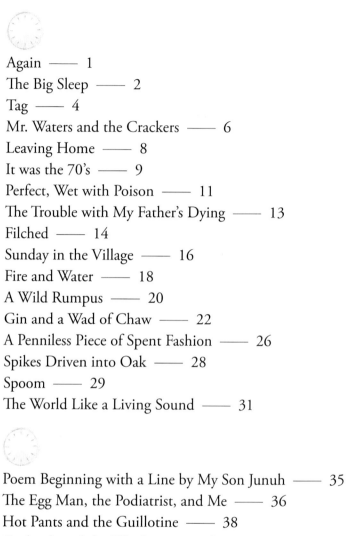

Father,
Did I, too,
Open your heart almost to breaking?
　　　　　—Thomas McGrath

Again

Gray clouds bluing into fog,
a dark season stretches

across windows full of empty panes
and the red bricks crumbling.

Through the pitched roof baring beams,
a small rain down does rain.

Love, again, I've lost you
and again, you've led me home.

The Big Sleep

I read it on the Greyhound   back before I saw Bogart in Marlowe's clothes,

    before the old man bought the Buick,

    before he changed to dust,

    before my mother scattered him

    beside a scrubby desert tree   along the highway to Lake Mead.

    Before I didn't buy the whiskey, before

    I didn't hoist a glass, before   I didn't tell the grandson

    he had never seen,

my father died, not knowing what names went with what faces.

Some hospital joe   wheeled him down the long, white hall,

    while Santa Anas   spilled desert across the town.

    While I ducked the rain in Brooklyn, my collar against the storm,
    sodden strangers   plunging with me to the train,
    an ambulance drove him slowly   to where the fires blaze,
    hot enough to roast   flesh and bone to scrap and ash.

    While undertakers readied   to fit him for the flames,
    I taught the book   that I had plucked
    from the rack beside his Lazy Boy.

He told me to take it, if I wanted.

He was done, tired of Chandler anyway.

On a fall day in Vegas, strong winds whipping in,

     tourists went on laying down their bets,

     showgirls continued   powdering their breasts,

     and the Lake Mead carp   still churned and flopped
     over each other, rubbery lips agape,
     for the popcorn thrown their way.

Tag

Waukegan Harbor with its view of Zion
nuclear plant and coast littered
with alewives, their six inches of silver
scattered before smoking lakeside silos,
was where we wandered and played
      a dead-fish tag,
flinging and firing them at one another
to cap an insult or fill too long a silence.

We roamed that blight without the coin
to bear us across, where we heard tell
      of loose-limbed girls
who sunned and dove, glistening,
into the wash of tide. Lake water
beading when they emerged, sleek
as the sheen of a showroom coupe.
White sand banking into dunes.

Jeff Niemi claimed to have traveled
      there without us
in his cousin's rusted-out LeMans.
Heaven, sh-e-e-e-r heaven, he sighed,
laying a palm to his burnt neck.
      Water so clear, I saw fish
      smaller than Tolan's dick
swim through the legs of one hot little mama.

Allied against his all too certain lies,
we bore what arms were given us
        and fired
the rank corpses that fit so nicely
into the empty pockets of our hands.
Bombarded, he wailed and snarled,
        fish-stung from the beach.

Our ammunition caked with sores,
we wiped our hands off on the sand,
        the sand off on our jeans,
and went on, half hearts denying
        all of us were *It*

Mr. Waters and the Crackers

Lewandowski, my buddy with the car-wash job,
calls too early on a weekend morning,

> *Get your hippy, vagrant, poet ass out of bed,*
> *if you want to meet the man.*

Lewandowski washed Muddy Waters' car,
an old mint-green Cadillac, cool as cash, Sundays on the side.

Lewandowski worked in yuppie Downers Grove,
and Waters would glide his long lozenge of a ride
over from Westmont to have her done up nice

until my pal brokered a deal
to be Waters' personal car-wash boy,
willing to make house calls on his day off
to have something to brag about over Sunday barbecue.

And I was being bestowed the honor of tagging along,
so I could back him up to the disbelievers,
though it promised to be a story for me as well.

I was hauling on my jeans and spitting out the Crest,
when Lewandowski pulled up in his Bondo-ed Barracuda,
playing the requisite Chicago blues only a little too loud.

After this chatty preamble, you might want me to draw
the yarn out for you with humor and perhaps
one passing moment of memorable delight.

But the truth is, the man just came out
to pay us when we were done, to look over our job
and see if it was worthy of his cash,

and Lewandowski, desperate as we both were
for something more, let leap from his white trash tongue

what shit it was those British Invasion bands had got their mitts
all over Mr. Waters' music and made millions,
while he had to live in some clapboard bungalow.

    Well, he said, *that's true, but the house is mine.*

    Caddie too.

    And now I got two skinny-ass crackers comin' to my house
    first thing on a Sunday mornin'
    to call me Mister *and have her done up nice.*

    Who'd a thought?

He peeled our few bucks off the roll he drew
from his crushed velvet robe
and strolled chuckling back into his house

as Lewandowski stared after him, and I wiped
one last smudge from the handle of his driver's side door.

Leaving Home

for James Wright

Eight years of Reagan, and our fathers slouched,
           hollow as robbed graves,
atop their bar stools daily. Union jobs long gone,
they were men of a dying age, chewing
the well-gnawed bones of how good they had it,
      when they hated the shift boss
and the shift, when they pulled too much overtime
at Anchor Hocking, Johns Manville, Abbott Labs.

What became of our once proud fathers—
      their flinty surrender to what they were
abandoned to remain in our industrial town—
          one among the reasons
we fled to what our haggard adolescence
could imagine of escape, of lives decent and full
of something more than beer and hope confounded.

Grubby, middling next-door neighbors to white trash,
      we drove late nights packed
like livestock into our fathers' wheezing rides
to scoop the loop and spy on those we envied
      for their happiness and ease
as they poured into places a man might lift a glass
to more than a life he never meant to love.

It was the 70's

and the carpets
were wall-to-wall. My mother
had a plastic rake
she used daily to keep the nap
of her green shag piled high.

After raking
the sin was to move around
and mash her plush.
For Christ's sake, Jimmy, can't you
stay put in one place? I just

raked the rug.
It was easier to head outside,
even on a January
afternoon already dark,
snow up to my knees,

and nothing
right or wrong to do. My dad,
home early
for once, found me lobbing
snowballs up onto the roof.

Whatcha doin'?
"Mom just raked the rug."
He nodded,
plucked a lump of snow,
squeezed and flung

                    a perfect strike
at the bird feeder planted
                twenty paces
deep into the yard. Put
a nice crack in the nearside

                    plate glass,
then packed another tight one
            that smelled faintly
of Luckies and handed it to me.
Have at it, kid. I'll cover you inside.

Perfect, Wet with Poison

At Edwards' Field, near the marsh, ours was the blood
the mosquitoes in their gangly stealth sought. At dusk
the city sent a truck, its sprinkler spraying
a cascade of malathion, foul line to foul line,
from out past the chain-link fence. Time called,

we spread our arms and turned like we'd been told,
spinning slow circles, left field to right
and across the infield dirt, the chemical
mist wafting over us, its sting
like sharp dew settling into the corners of our eyes.

The umpire tossed a dry ball to the tall boy on the hill,
who rubbed it slowly between bare hands
as he peered up at the crowd. The drumming in his ears
dulling to a drone, he stepped to the rubber
and leaned in. No runners to check, hadn't been all game.

Where but here was perfect even possible
for a gawky boy with elbows thicker than his arms?
Glove to chest, fingers to four seams, blow out.
Fielders pounding their mitts, chanting and swaying.
The gloam falling across the mound. And in the stands

his mother done with her cursing of the city and its truck.
Chapped hands over her stung eyes, she didn't see
her boy kick high and hurl one
sharp-eyed home. Only heard the hush before
the leather popped and those around her rose.

Her husband roared with all the rest
before he dropped a hand
to her bent back and with the other waved.
Caught his long son's gaze, clenched a fist
and beamed before their boy was swarmed.

Then sat down, leaned in, angled for her ear.
His right hand at her elbow, she lifted
her eyes at last to gather in
the ruckus their son's left arm had wrought.
Worry later, Mary Lou. Stand up and let him see you proud.

The Trouble with My Father's Dying

is not that it is done, not
that I didn't wrap my useless arms
around his useless corpse.

The trouble is
I didn't reach my hands into his
last days of breathing

and touch the him
he might in dying have finally
given me to hold

like his child in my arms.

Filched

Is that vintage? they ask.

It was my father's, I say and think of a man for whom
that word meant only a crack about drink—

> *Gimme a tall one of your finest vintage!*

I found it among tie pins and cufflinks in his top drawer,
filched it years before I knew the word,

> knew only that I wanted something I could take from him
> who knew work and the bar better than home,

> something I would have never called
> *beautiful* and *ruined.*

Crystal scratched, leather dry and stitching frayed.
He never noticed it was gone,

> or else he never said.

From his dresser to the carved wooden box I buried
inside my hand-me-down chest,

> until the no more of him sent me rooting
> for some relic I could hold.

Glass polished and gears set right, new band strapped around my wrist.

Vintage?

It's beautiful, they say.

It was my father's, and I let them assume,

inheritance or gift,

that he was a man of taste, who shared it with his son.

Sunday in the Village

Junuh at six needs to pee, inconvenient
before we stumble on an inn, votive-lit
and peopled by a small congregation of regulars,
familiar as memory pooling back to light.

The barkeep pauses from his ablutions.
I nod to my son at the end of my right arm.
He smirks and nods, returns to his towel and glass.

Relieved, Junuh washes his hands and asks
how I knew my way to the toilet without asking.

I tell him his grandfather loved a place
just like this back in Illinois, brought me there
Sundays as a boy to watch the Cubs, drink
Shirley Temples, and twirl the stool beneath me.

He asks if we can stay. I order him
extra cherries, teach him to spin a stool
and answer the men at the bar when they ask
the usual kindnesses—his name, how old,
so big, what sort of ball he likes to play.

Will ya look at that blond hair? Those eyes a' yours,
I suppose they're blue. Yes, sir, this one's gonna be
a real lady killer.

No, the quiet one chimes in.
Junuh will be a gentleman and a scholar. Won't you, son?

Gentleman and scholar, words I'd heard so many times
from my father's mouth, his highest praise for a man
and his hope for me.

                Junuh nods and says his *Yes, sir,*
to the bespectacled man, who winks and grins
as he sips his olived gin, shaken with vermouth.

I smile his way, greet his eyes, before I buy
us all another round, a little more time
in this dim dream to toast the living and the dead.

Fire and Water

1.

It was late, just three of us that night
at the pool the rich kids owned by day,
and Hakko the first to hear
the thwonk and wobble of the board.

Near the chain link we caught sight
of the O'Reilly boys,
fire in their mouths as they dove—

        cannonball, belly flop, swan
        and dead man's plunge—

their concert tees and boot-cut jeans
clinging to teenage scrawn.

They were lighting twenty at a time
chomped between their teeth.
Pack after pack into a brother's mouth,
lit then doused in the pool.

We watched them finish a carton off,
pull on their high tops and climb
out under the spotlight opposite us,
spent smokes bobbing in their wake.

2.

We didn't swim that night amid their mess,
but Schmo was on the horn
first thing next morning.

Shawn and Jeff, the O'Reilly boys,
their dad had flipped a rail that night
in his wicked GTO, didn't make it
breathing to the ambulance.

He was the last we knew who took
his smokes unfiltered, Pall Malls
he bought from my mom down at the Jewel
one flame-red carton at a time.

A Wild Rumpus

When I was ten, we moved to our first house,
and I followed the raucous sound of boys
past ball fields and off into a snatch of prairie.

There two teams—each behind its own barricade
of shopping carts, warped plywood, milk crates,
and bedspreads stiff with stains—threw all array of balls—

        tennis and dodge,
        base- and soft-,
        wet Nerf
        and sagging soccer,
        footballs
        like sunken
        bladders bereft of air.

It seemed to me, a child used to playing alone,
a wild rumpus in a heaven of boys
set loose in the tall, summer grasses.

The crane-like one with the bowl-cut hair
called me whooping to his team, as the others,
who'd been hoarding weapons, charged

in a barrage of balls. My team, caught
not unaware, responded with an onslaught
of dirt clods, sticks, and flying tackles.

While the boy named Tock beside me ran
off with a sloshing, repurposed Hellman's jar,
I veered for the cover of clumped saplings

some few yards away. He doused
the unguarded enemy fortifications
with the contents of that quart

then torched it with a Bic. My team
commenced to hooting and high stepping.
Even the losers joined in, two armies

circling the flames. This the happiest
I'd ever seen sober people be: boys disarmed
around a fire lapping blankets and dry wood.

Angels of infernos and safe distance,
be as kind to my boy. Lead him to joy
and sanctuary from joy burst into flame.

Gin and a Wad of Chaw

Hunky Drinkwine's brother Billy
let me pull a plug of chaw
to round my cheek and widen
my eye, just like a real ballplayer.

Three batters in, I had it down—

        lean over, take the sign and nod.
        Pause, hands to chest, spit
        a nice brown stream to first
        and fire home—

until he showed in the bottom of the fifth.

My dad had left the bar to see me throw
but if he saw me chewing too,
he was likely to march his drunkenness
out to the mound, cuff me by the neck
and haul me stumbling home.

I shifted my gob far side and set
myself not to spit. But willfulness alone
can't keep a wad of chew
stuffed in a boy's moist cheek
from draining down his throat.

 I dragged wet fingers across my chest
not waiting to take the sign
just catch and hurl it home.

I made it through the first two,
when Tommy Voight came up
with his bright idea

and kept raising
his hand
to the ump,

stepping out,
adjusting
his helmet and

his cup,
situating
his grip,

smirking
and staring
my way.

I spent all kinds of forever
on the rubber, bent
over my front knee, waiting—

pitch   after   pitch

—for him to step back in,

I got wild before I went pale, before
I lurched and spewed
a septic-colored gusher
all over the front side of the hill.

The ump and catcher rushed out
followed by my coach. Teammates
began to circle but
I waved them off and started
kicking dirt over the mess.

Some dad brought out a bucket
of sand and a rake. Quick enough,
the world was nearly good as new.

Coach and ump worried over me
but I wasn't coming out. My father
didn't budge, a pillar in the stands—
his stare, when I checked him
from my pause, blinkless and glued.

The catcher put a finger down
and set up tight inside.

I heaved one behind Tommy
that caught him in the hip.

He couldn't say much
just threw me a look
and gimped his way to first.

Robbie Tock, a full
bat length off the plate, saw
three darts, each taller than the last,
till the third had him flailing
up around his neck.

Inning over, I marched myself
out through centerfield
into the long, dry grass,

until I found the tree shanty
the Adams boys had built
to enjoy their father's cigarettes and porn.

The night was clear—
just a clipped nail of moon
and stars that pricked the dark.

Insects chirped and droned
as I lay down against warped wood,
a story above the ground, wanting only

a piece of gum to take the taste
of bile and tobacco from my tongue
and the good luck he'd sleep off
that day's memories and gin.

A Penniless Piece of Spent Fashion

Who wears my father's face today,
a man miscast before the weather,
rain-splattered and sure he is unloved?

Who huddles beneath the cold and gray
as north wind bitter slants sharp rain
against the tattered sway of him?

Who wants dry clothes, stiff drink to warm
and unweary his besotted bones,
an ear to fill with liquored yarn?

Who on grim earth alone would wage
a moment's hope on a needle's-eye
chance of resurrection? The son,

whose seeming father stands,
begging each mortal hand and eye
for what small mercies fall his way,

whose cup of coins becomes his wine,
his heart as mine, faithless and forlorn,
forgetful of what follows rain,

who shades the sun's return. Forgiveness
and the muddy-footed crow sent to claw
some clay of hope from a life interred,

who finds land the too-white dove demurred
and knows this rain-soaked creature,
famished and loosed to squalor,

whose tartared gaze I catch before I crush
a twenty crisp into his leathered hand.
Rummy eyes, the crusted corners of his grin.

Spikes Driven into Oak

He must have come alone at night –
no mercenary soul to squawk
the story of what would seem the moon-
dropped madness of a man who knew
only bold and repeated injury could save
what would otherwise become
barrel, box, or beam, and not
the final pillar of a cathedral's ruin.

To be wise you must do more than know
the hum of sap within your timbre
or an oak's. You must own
the strength to drive spike after spike
into the fragrant body of what you love.
To save it from another's necessity and saw.

Spoom

Ted Stein, who had been dying slowly,
is now quickly dying

and wants to write *one really good poem.*

The chemo and narcotics make it difficult,
muddle his once clear mind.

For what will be his last workshop,
Ted finds an old word

and uses it in a poem no better than dying.

Now he is certain he will never write
that one good poem.

I, without prognosis yet, ask if I can use

the word he has discovered
like an island no one inhabits anymore.

Ted says, *Sure.* Tells me,
Go ahead, without resentment or joy

but resignation that he will die
without one good poem to his name.

I lay a hand to his shoulder, bend
my knees to thank him eye to eye.

He lifts his gaze, a moment

and bequeaths to me that word
he might still save, tells me

to write *something as good as breathing.*

The World Like a Living Sound

The silence after
this white sustenance of snow different than
the hush before the late night storm.

> *Call yourself alive? I promise you*
> *the world like a living sound.*

Cassian, Kumin, Emerson, Kinnell,
Kizer, Heaney, Strand.

> *Nothing is changed except*
> *there was a moment when*
> *the wolf, who stands*
> *outside the self*
> *lay lightly down, and slept,*

After darkness,
the slow, soft flakes
covering Manhattan's asphalt and concrete.

> *her shadow, moving with us,*
> *that dark, that soft, the gray*
> *that seeks out winter's cloth*

The spiked city's canyons clad in white.

> *as if it will be*
> *only a small dislocation*
> *to pass from this paradise to the next.*

Poet after poet gone
by December's end,
              nothing
that doesn't rise remains

We are meant to be stripped down,
to prepare us for something better,
so you may write this poem

              only the fallen
              snow, inescapable,
              silent as the sheets that cloak

out of the marvellous as you have known it

              the bodies of the dead, the white
              that shrouds them all.

and find in that final flowing
of cold through your limbs
that you love what you are…

What awaits the heart
if Love bears no arrows?
　　　—Federico García Lorca

Poem Beginning with a Line by My Son Junuh

Every head should have a body.

Every body
          a soul the size
                    of a jukebox loaded

with tunes our bodies know without us.

My hips begin
          to remember
                    the pleasure I was born to

my mouth to hum the songs I never knew

I didn't know.
          My body
                    moving alone among others moving

and singing until I am one with the other

bodies
          my soul sings to.
                    Each honkytonk hymn making holy

what my head forgot to love.

The Egg Man, the Podiatrist, and Me

My grandmother carried half pieces of Wrigley's gum in her purse,
      Doublemint for the cold months,
        Juicy Fruit for the warm.
Every other Friday she would dress for her podiatrist,
swathing the still-smooth skin behind her knees
in Tabu, her most extravagant dime-store cologne.
        Only once was there a problem with her feet.

And then there was Nello, the egg man who wooed her
with his weathered, picket-fence grin,
        free cream for her coffee,
        a weekly dozen on the side.
Once, after he slipped me a Kennedy half dollar
on the way back to his truck, my mother asked
        how I'd like an egg man for a grandfather.

I watched my grandmother's furrowed, horn-rimmed gaze
        drop from her daughter to me.
        Once Catholic, twice divorced,
she looked at me with pity wearied by scorn,
No offense, Jimmy, but men are only good for one thing,
and I'm getting too old even for that anymore.

I nodded, no less confused, before she offered
        a half piece of stale winter gum,
        its torn edge dusted with dark lint.
The gum shattered into pieces against my teeth
        but fell back together over time.

I was grateful for her shard of sugar, grateful
as the foot doctor and egg man must have been
before she grew too spent to rouse
sweetness from her tattered bag,
which she unclasped in old age
only for us three.

Hot Pants and the Guillotine

I doubt my desire extended
        beyond an appetite for air
free from the mentholated haze
        of my mother's Kool 100s.

But when I poked my head out the back
        of our '72 Chevy four-door,
                window wide
to the assault of August heat,

        carhops glided past.
                The long muscles
of their thighs and calves, taut lines
above four wheels, cotton piping straining

as they lightly lunged and rolled. One arm
        like Lady Liberty above them,
                the other,
brushing fenders and making change.

Without a glance, my mother raised
        the power window
from which I ogled. My craned neck
pinched between glass and frame,

I bug-eyed toward the one that I loved best,
                coasting our way
in her roller-derby-hot-pants beneficence,
        embossed name tag gleaming,

Theresa as she approached.
She tapped on the shut window
      of the shotgun seat.
My mother gestured driver's side.

Your son! Theresa yelled. My mother
           twisted slowly
    around and laughed, pointed me,
guillotined but whole, out to my father, while

I clung to the glass and groaned
           longingly toward Theresa.
   The window lowered and I coughed
too audibly and clutched my dented throat.

Quit hammin' it up, my mother rasped
before she barked Theresa's way,
         Gimme a root beer, kid,
   then handed it to me.

Take a sip. You're fine. Don't make
      such a commotion outta nothin'.
Theresa peered in as I chugged and gave me
        a quick wink and a grin

before she wheeled off and left me
        cradling my mug,
    slick with sweat
and half-drunk between my knees.

Cocktails and the Weather

Where moist pressure meets bright sky,
dark clouds weigh a heavy rain.

Steam rising from the city's crust
and clotted pores, we slide

fingers and thumbs
in tandem, trailing

the condensation of our drinks.
Pedestal to stem,

her fingers slip to where
her goblet makes its perch, linger

then stroke from there
to base and back again.

I touch a finger to the damp
rim of my glass

and slowly circle.
We watch

each other watching
each other's trace and glide,

fingers slick
with the sweat heat draws from cool

before thunder announces light,
before rain succumbs to storm.

The Logic of My Ecstasy and Faith

That you deliver me to rapture fraught
with screams the neighbors
have taken to greeting with applause

through walls that otherwise maintain
our civil silence
presupposes two possible causes:

either your labia are the pearly gates
redesigned by St. Peter
out of his uncommon love for me

and frame the halls of Heaven wherein
angels in flight along the girded length of me
celebrate the glory of our Lord,

or such heaven is mere deceit,
and the feathers are from among the fallen
now residing in the heat you keep below.

The Bible does not clarify. Our priest tells me
to count my blessings, so I am resigned
to being a moral man no more, unconcerned

with whose kingdom I visit within yours,
thankful instead for the angels you offer me
regardless of theology and my eternal soul.

These two

　　　　　　　　　pairs of shoes—

one　　　　　large and brown

the other　　　small and black—

that have traipsed　　the dusty

four corners　　of their worlds

belong now　　together in this house.

Terror in the Service of Delight

From the taxidermist who specialized in alligator heads
priced by the inch, I toted a stuffed bullfrog to her house,
stowed inside a brown paper sack I gave to her daughter,
nearly five and still inclined to let me in the door.

> *This is a present for your mom,*
> *a surprise I want you to hide till later, but,*
> *whatever you do, don't peak inside.*

A few steps out of the room, I heard the thrilling scream
of innocence disheveled. Her mother, not yet accustomed
to such high-pitched joy, darted for the stairs.

Jewel's hands framed the outskirts of her face.
Sack open at her feet, she pointed there.

Her mother peered inside then puckered her grimace my way.

I smirked and gathered the gift returned to me
that became for years a paperweight on my desk,
where Jewel brought friends to prove
her story of my depravity was true.

They stared but, like apt princesses, wouldn't touch
its dried but slimy-seeming hide.

Some mustered courage in the guise of indignation
and asked if I really handed this ham hock-sized
atrocity over to their unsuspecting friend.

I played the part I was invited to reprise
and looked each with wanton glee dead in the eye,

I really did.

Some wanted answers, others wagged their heads
and left me, irredeemable in their wake,
arm round my stepdaughter's level shoulder
as they turned her from my lair.

                                    Most times,
she glanced back and grinned, sometimes at me,
more often at *that frog*, my first best gift to her.

Supposed to

Better are the days misspent as this, where,
instead of what I'm supposed to do,
I write these words, or better, and implore
you in a hush to fuck me like I'd just
come home from a war

to which tomorrow I return. Worse and more frequent
are the days of YouTube, Facebook, solitaire,
repeat, instead of the work that has to be but
not yet, just not yet, and I, like you, know
it would be better to be done with it

and have what time remains for what we love,
for the words and respites from war, perfect
al fresco cappuccinos between,
brimming with froth. The sun and strolls unencumbered,
the garden we still tend to promise each other,
the cooking of what pleases, the laughter
among friends at the little hells we raise,

but—always this *but*, regret
never worthy of a story, the *but*
of the lists piled insidious before us,
capable of worming like the spiritual
slither of an opiate malaise—those

powers with which we're left, good only
for scrolling across webbed ether to the next
window this weariness demands. The stupors

that possess and transform us into those

we don't know, the interminable dread
of dying into what we are supposed
to do, of convincing ourselves that what
we are ineffectually committed to
supposing makes us worthy of our lives.

Conjecture

More than the execution
of what we owe
to whom and for how long,

more than attention
swallowed and returned,

love might be the kindness
that bathes the crust from life

like scalding milk
and a wire brush
to thick and brutish hides.

Eros Regardless

after Sappho

          I, who made with her our home
a hell of bickering and small cruelties, had
little will to discern love's full terror till
the menace of desire spread
               thin flames beneath my skin:

creature of rutting, famished for flesh,
loosener of limbs, sweetbitter
               animal that gave rise
to me who did not choose it
         but couldn't bear that ache for long.

Those whirling wolves within us came
               to furrow our soft sheets
and return the musk of heat to scorn
until the wet we made beneath us dried
         into a continent between us.

Threadbare

My one and only wants to know how I could be so riled
when all she said to that buff and tatted biker was   *Hello.*

Even fools like the one she plays, or the one she plays me for,
know—more than words—her slantwise eyes and her
moist lips command the moment of a greeting.

Accused, she rolls what had been slant and turns
her jeans, snug as lacquer, to the door –
cherried ash straggling thin plumes as she struts.

What his leathered, wind-blown body knows of her
Hello takes me by the throat and tears
my soft lungs from me, churns the blood between my ears,

and mows what once was ripe, when I was he, and she
made the world in which we kissed.

Singers and Sacks of Tar

The end of us begun,
my wife sang

what my longing didn't know
it longed to hear—

silence overwhelmed
by slow pain that still knew joy—

a blues somewhere between
birdsong and Billie.

My pit packed thick with pitch,
that song

found no emptiness
in me to hold it

and she left me
for a man more hollow

whose pierced ribs were
the bone strings of his heart.

Who we were
became what each remembered.

Who I was
sewed the sheets we'd shared

into the sacks I used to haul
black years of tar from me

and make from nothing
resurrected

the air
a voice could fill

with songs
to pare the corners from the moon.

While I Complained—

enamored with the succulence
of my misery and contempt—

how my wife had been laying down
steady rhythms with her bass player,

picking my pocket and letting him
play her harp for free,

my friend, her engineer—

lips set and head gently bobbing
to the babbling of my incessant laments—

turned to queue a new track on his system.

Before I recognized it was hers—
the pitch-perfect a capella

she laid down for me,
Greensleeves, lullaby of our end—

my bitch and moan caught in my throat
and set my every ounce to trembling.

That voice I still loved drew
the sting of salt from me

and quieted all except what was
most true and impossible to say.

The Hobgoblins of My Slumber
Raise the Gallows of Her Face

My former   death-do-us-part   returned last night
to pull from her   black wedding gown the thread
with which she wound me   about her least left finger
—pale spool raveling the strand—before she drew
it round her throat   in hangman's choker   before
she whirled   her pout and moon-drunk eyes
before she tied   its slender midnight to the plunge
and blush   of her blowsy collar   and   moist-lipped
she purred

    I might just let you   get me out of this

You Clipped the Waves, Delilah—

the ones you loved to clutch
as you pulled me
gasping to your mouth—

and made of those locks
a bracelet braided
with painted beads to ride
the skin of your thin wrist.

You wore it everywhere

      even to the ocean
      of another's bed

before you came back to me,

bald at the wrist, and
like the soft drape
of my hair, mine

no more.

I've Shopped for Years These Cold Cases Empty Tonight: Nocturne with Butcher and Lycanthrope

The night manager in his blood-smeared apron loads

unmarked parcels
into a brown bag
for no one who is there.

> *Hunger feeds on fatted flesh*
> *grave-eyed*
> *beneath the cresting moon.*

> *Coarse hair rises at such light.*

I ask about the dearth
of customary cuts
upon which

> *the moist-flesh moan*
> *for meat and marrow,*

I have come to depend. He assures me

> *Eyes fatten on a throat left bare.*

all I have come to expect

> *A tongue lolls from grizzled chops.*

is as available to me, now as it ever was.

> *Such wailing*
> *before the low growl of the kill.*

I need only ask.

> *The howl*
> *before what need be done.*

He nods and begins to place
plain, white paper packages

into the serrated
mouths of bags along the counter.

> *The great grip of the jaw.*

> *Growl gone*
> *to blood song in the throat.*

My Fair Daddy

My son wants me to stop singing
while I scrub the knives
holding their little scraps of meat.

What's wrong with you?
You sound
like a chicken with a toothache.

He's eight and has no idea
the plethora of simple arts
I butcher daily.

Soon he will grow more
appalled by my ever
more obvious lacks.

For now he's willing
to tender me hope
like a line of household credit.

No-o-o, he says, nabbing me
stiff-hipped but bopping
to Mos Def in our kitchen.

When you bust that move,
you have to look
down at your belly.

I comply and glide
for a few moments like a man
with almost slanky flanks.

Junuh grins and we flounce *to the bang*
to the boogie say up jump the boogie
to the rhythm of the boogie to be.

Quiet Dog simmers down,
and we return, Junuh
to the toy soldiers he aligns

in bloodless battles
across the living room floor,
and I to the teeth of our knives.

Junuh at Nine

My son has begun to set out on his own,
to form allegiances with friends
whose secrets he, by age-old code,
          is compelled to keep.
His world more and more his alone.

Already, Jordan has broken a boy's arm.
Daquan was caught at recess with a blade.
Jesse pummeled Andre. And Junuh
          has no idea how
his new fake leather coat was torn.

I can no longer expect him to tell me all
and still become who he needs to be.
Walking to the seamstress, I tell him
          how it's easy
most times to fix a coat, harder to patch

an ornery, fair-skinned boy. I look at the scar
from when he fell walking the dogs at two.
He squinches his lips, gives me a quick
          wallop to the gut
and runs, laughing, victorious, away.

The MRI

Inside this grave
womb that drums
and groans
as it takes

picture
after
picture
of my spine

I hear it
seem to say

go   /   you go

don't   /   you go

don't go   /   don't

go now   /   don't

I'm 52, inside
this calibrated tube, this
picture box
and singing machine

that will tell
my doctors if
the drugs and
transplanted

marrow have
been killing
the tumors set
on killing me

go / *don't grow*

don't / *go*

The droning
chant of this
temporary tomb
returns me

to Junuh at the ocean
only four
and screaming
into the waves

the two of us
charging, arms
flailing like
the fleshy swords they are

the water beating us
back before
we *Charge!* again,
roaring the whole time.

We can't give up. We
have to fight, he says.
And back we go
wild into the wake.

don't go / *don't*

go / *don't*

go now / *grow*

grow / *you*

grow / *no*

don't / *go*

don't / *grow*

go / *no*

Afterword

Spirit

Every head should have a body.
How else can you dance?

Some people dance the Jippity Jig
or the Hoppity Row.

The fireflies dance with the stars
that have no names.

But you dance differently.
You dance with the snow flakes

going where the wind tells you.
No worries. No goals. Just dreams to lead you.

by Junuh Tolan, 11

ABOUT THE AUTHOR

JAMES TOLAN (1964-2017) is the author of *Mass of the Forgotten* (Autumn House Press), *Red Walls* (Dos Madres Press) and co-editor with Holly Messitt of *New America: Contemporary Literature for a Changing Society* (Autumn House Press). He lived in Brooklyn and taught at the Borough of Manhattan Community College/City University of New York.

His website is www.jamestolan.com.

Author photo by Tina Schula

Other books by James Tolan
published by Dos Madres Press

Red Walls (2011)

He is also included in:
Realms of the Mothers:
The First Decade of Dos Madres Press - 2016

For the full Dos Madres Press catalog:
www.dosmadres.com